MIDLOTHIAN PUBLIC LIBRARY

3 1614 00200 9729

W9-CNO-272

ORAL HISTORIES

MIDLOTHIAN PUBLIC LIBRARY
14701 S. KENTON AVENUE
MIDLOTHIAN, IL 60445

BY AGATHA GREGSON

Gareth Stevens
PUBLISHING

Please visit our website, www.garethstevens.com. For a free color catalog of all our high-quality books, call toll free 1-800-542-2595 or fax 1-877-542-2596.

Library of Congress Cataloging-in-Publication Data

Names: Gregson, Agatha.
Title: Oral histories / Agatha Gregson.
Description: New York : Gareth Stevens Publishing, 2020. | Series: Cultures connect us! | Includes index.
Identifiers: LCCN 2018042001| ISBN 9781538238509 (pbk.) | ISBN 9781538238523 (library bound) | ISBN 9781538238516 (6-pack)
Subjects: LCSH: Oral history–Juvenile literature.
Classification: LCC D16.14 .G735 2020 | DDC 907.2–dc23
LC record available at https://lccn.loc.gov/2018042001

Published in 2020 by
Gareth Stevens Publishing
111 East 14th Street, Suite 349
New York, NY 10003

Copyright © 2020 Gareth Stevens Publishing

Designer: Reann Nye
Editor: Therese Shea

Photo credits: series art (background) Lukasz Szwaj/Shutterstock.com; cover imtmphoto/Shutterstock.com; p. 5 India Picture/Shutterstock.com; p. 7 Antracit/Shutterstock.com; p. 9 Oleinik Iuliia/Shutterstock.com; p. 11 CREATISTA/Shutterstock.com; p. 13 track5/E+/Getty Images; p. 15 https://commons.wikimedia.org/wiki/File:Lange-MigrantMother02.jpg; p. 17 Hulton Archive/Getty Images; p. 19 Monkey Business Images/Shutterstock.com; p. 21 wavebreakmedia/Shutterstock.com.

All rights reserved. No part of this book may be reproduced in any form without permission in writing from the publisher, except by a reviewer.

Printed in the United States of America

CPSIA compliance information: Batch #CS19GS: For further information contact Gareth Stevens, New York, New York at 1-800-542-2595.

CONTENTS

Boldface words appear in the glossary.

Passing It On

Thousands of years ago, there were no written languages. People of every **culture** passed on **information** by telling it to others. This is called the **oral** tradition. It allowed information to be remembered for a long, long time.

Some information was in the form of stories such as legends. These tales may not have been totally true, but they were used to teach lessons, explain why things happened, or pass on a value. Other stories were about events that really happened. They're a kind of oral history.

Preserving History

Oral histories are people's real-life **experiences**. They help us understand historical times better. Modern historians believe oral histories should be recorded, not just spoken or written down by others. Recording an oral history is a way of **preserving** people's memories exactly.

Have you ever **repeated** someone else's story? You probably changed some of the words. The longer the story, the harder it is to remember its **details**. That's another reason to record oral histories with **technology** such as smartphones, computers, and video cameras.

The Interview

An oral history can come from anyone. The person doesn't have to be rich or famous. When recording an oral history, a person often **interviews** another person. The interviewer makes sure to record many details about the other person's experiences.

Famous Oral Histories

In 1935, the US government created the Federal Writers' Project. As part of it, ordinary people were interviewed about their lives. Many people were suffering at this time because of the **Great Depression**. We know about their lives because of oral histories.

Former slaves were also interviewed for the Federal Writers' Project. More than 2,300 oral histories of slavery were collected. It's important to know what slaves experienced during this terrible time in US history. We can learn about their lives best through their own words.

17

Make Oral History!

You can record the oral history of someone in your community. Your grandparents or other older people often have great stories. Write down questions you want to ask about a past event. Record your interview with a smartphone or other recording tool.

Hidden History

Many history books talk about wars and other major world events. However, they don't tell us much about how they affected regular people's lives. Oral histories help preserve the history of our communities and cultures—and people like you!

GLOSSARY

culture: the beliefs and ways of life of a group of people

detail: a small part

experience: something that you have done or that has happened to you

Great Depression: a period of economic troubles with widespread unemployment and poverty (1929–1939)

information: knowledge obtained from study or observation

interview: to question someone in order to get information or learn about that person. Also, the written or taped record of the meeting.

oral: spoken

preserve: to keep something in its original state

repeat: to make, do, or say something again

technology: tools, machines, or ways to do things that use the latest discoveries to fix problems or meet needs

FOR MORE INFORMATION

BOOKS

Barghoorn, Linda. *Be a Speech Detective*. New York, NY: Crabtree Publishing Company, 2017.

Yasuda, Anita. *Oral Traditions and Storytelling*. Collingwood, ON: Beech Street Books, 2018.

WEBSITES

Step-by-Step Guide to Oral History

dohistory.org/on_your_own/toolkit/oralHistory.html
Learn much more about how to record an oral history.

What Is Oral History?

historymatters.gmu.edu/mse/oral/what.html
Read more about what is—and isn't—oral history.

Publisher's note to educators and parents: Our editors have carefully reviewed these websites to ensure that they are suitable for students. Many websites change frequently, however, and we cannot guarantee that a site's future contents will continue to meet our high standards of quality and educational value. Be advised that students should be closely supervised whenever they access the internet.

INDEX

24